WOW.
That Was A
BIG
Emotion.

A Socemo Story by Amy Williams

Please do not reproduce, distribute or transmit in any form or by any means, including photocopying, recording, or any other method without the prior written permission of the author except in the case of short quotations for reviews and other noncommercial uses permitted by copyright law.

For permission requests, please write to the author.

For bulk purchases, or to make a Socemo Book request, please reach out to Amy at amywilliamsacademy.com

Text & design © 2022

For all the children who inspired countless Socemo Books and to the AWA Square Squad: Dana, Shazia, Mary, Abby, Millie & Craig.

Special thanks to Millie Williams for text artistry!

NOTE TO THE IMPORTANT ADULTS:

WHAT IS A SOCEMO BOOK? IT IS A STORY TO SHARE AGAIN AND AGAIN WITH YOUR CHILD THAT COVERS SOCIAL-EMOTIONAL TOPICS. THINK OF IT AS A 'HOW TO DO THINGS' STORY.

THIS BOOK IS BEST READ TOGETHER--ADULT & CHILD--SO YOU CAN SHARE WHEN YOU FELT THE SAME WAY OR WHEN THE SAME THING HAPPENED TO YOU. SOMETIMES DIVING INTO TOPICS LIKE THIS CAN BRING BACK FEELINGS AND MEMORIES OF YOUR OWN CHILDHOOD.

BE BRAVE AND SHARE HOW YOU FELT AND WHAT YOU DID WHEN YOU WERE LEARNING HOW TO REGULATE YOUR OWN EMOTIONS. THIS WILL DEEPEN THE CONNECTION BETWEEN YOU AND YOUR CHILD AND REMIND THEM THAT THEY ARE NOT ALONE.

YOU GOT THIS!
-AMY

WOW.
That Was A
BIG
Emotion.

A Socemo Story about big feelings

by Amy Williams

I HAVE MANY KINDS OF FEELINGS.

SOMETIMES HAPPY.

SOMETIMES EXCITED

SOMETIMES SAD.

SOMETIMES ANNOYED.

SOMETIMES FRUSTRATED.

SOMETIMES

MAD.

SOMETIMES, MORE THAN ONE FEELING AT A TIME.

I CAN FEEL IT IN MY BODY.

MY FACE.

MY SHOULDERS.

MY CHEST.

MY LEGS.

SOMETIMES IT CAN FEEL

WARM.

SOMETIMES IT CAN FEEL

REALLY HOT.

SOMETIMES TIGHT.

SOMETIMES SHAKY.

SOMETIMES STILL.

IT IS OK TO HAVE ANY OF THESE FEELINGS.

THEY WON'T LAST FOREVER, ALTHOUGH SOMETIMES IT FEELS LIKE THEY WILL.

I CAN HELP MYSELF AND OTHERS.

I CAN ASK FOR HELP

WHEN I NEED IT.

SOMETIMES,

I FEEL HAPPY.

I FEEL CONTENT.

I FEEL CALM.

I HAVE FUN DOING MY WORK.

I AM HAVING FUN WITH MY FRIENDS.

I FOLLOW DIRECTIONS RIGHT AWAY.

MY BODY AND MIND ARE PEACEFUL.

THIS FEELS PRETTY GOOD.

SOMETIMES, I CAN NOTICE MY FEELINGS GETTING

BIGGER!

&

BIGGER!!

&

BIGGER

&

BIGGER

!!!

SOME THINGS ARE STARTING TO ANNOY ME, BUT I CAN STILL CONCENTRATE.

I MAY BE MOVING MORE S L O W L Y

BUT I CAN STILL LEARN AND PLAY.

I CAN MAKE A CHOICE TO HELP MYSELF FEEL BETTER!

I CAN TAKE A BREAK.

I CAN TAKE DEEP BREATHS.

I CAN GET SOME WATER.

THIS CAN MAKE THE FEELING SETTLE AND I CAN FEEL CALM AGAIN.

SOMETIMES, THESE FEELINGS, BEGIN TO GROW.

AND GROW...

IT IS GETTING HARDER TO STAY CALM AND FRIENDLY. MY MUSCLES FEEL TIGHT.

I CAN MAKE A CHOICE TO HELP MYSELF FEEL BETTER, BUT IT IS A LITTLE BIT HARDER.

HERE'S WHAT I CAN DO.

___ I can take a break.

___ I can take a deep breath.

___ I can get some water.

___ I can move my body.

___ I can play with a friend.

WOAH.

THE FEELINGS ARE GETTING

BIGGER AND BIGGER!

I AM NOT CALM NOR AM I FRIENDLY.

I AM NOT LEARNING.

I FEEL SO UPSET THAT I REALLY WANT

TO SCREAM OR KICK OR HIT.

MY MUSCLES FEEL VERY TIGHT NOW.

"IT IS TIME TO ASK AN ADULT TO HELP ME STAY CALM AND SAFE."

THEY CAN HELP ME FIGURE OUT WHAT TO DO.
THEY CAN HELP ME FEEL CALM, SAFE, AND HAPPY.

WHO ARE THE ADULTS THAT I CAN ASK FOR HELP?

1. _____

2. _____

3. _____

4. _____

5. _____

SOMETIMES, THE FEELING GETS SO BIG THAT IT...

EXPLODES!

SO VERY BIG AND VERY STRONG!
MY MUSCLES FEEL
VERY, VERY TIGHT.

IT DOESN'T FEEL GOOD AT ALL.

I FEEL VERY SAD,
OR I FEEL VERY
MAD.

I FEEL LIKE CRYING OR
KICKING, SCRATCHING OR
SCREAMING.

SOMETIMES, I MIGHT JUST DO THOSE THINGS AND FEEL EVEN WORSE.

I AM NOT FOLLOWING DIRECTIONS OR BEING SAFE WITH MY WORDS OR MY BODY.

I MAY FEEL embarrassed OR EVEN SCARED AT THE SAME TIME.

IT MAY BE THE FIRST TIME I HAVE EVER FELT THIS FEELING IN SUCH A BIG WAY.

MY FRIENDS WANT TO HELP WHEN I FEEL THIS WAY.

BUT IT IS BEST FOR AN ADULT TO HELP.

THEY CAN HELP ME FEEL CALM, SAFE, AND HAPPY.

Who are the adults that can help me when the feeling becomes so very big?

1. _____

2. _____

3. _____

4. _____

5. _____

EVERYONE HAS EMOTIONS

BIG

and small.

No matter how strong
my feelings get, I can do my best
to stay safe and calm.

I will have many kinds of feelings.

Sometimes happy.

Sometimes excited.

Sometimes sad.

Sometimes annoyed.

Sometimes frustrated.

Sometimes mad.

Sometimes more than one feeling at a time.

I AM HUMAN,
SO I WILL HAVE
MANY KINDS
OF FEELINGS.

IT IS OK TO HAVE ANY OF THESE FEELINGS.

Part of being human is feeling all of the feelings at one time or another, even the big ones will not last forever.

I CAN HELP MYSELF AND OTHERS.

I CAN ASK FOR HELP
WHEN I NEED IT.

Notes to all the important adults in the lives of children:

- Have this conversation when everyone is calm.
- Role model by naming when you feel a big feeling and what you are doing to help yourself feel calm again.
- Remind your child that all feelings are important and that it is part of being human. Big feelings don't last forever.
- This is important.

You got this!

Share your thoughts! Tell someone, share a photo or give this book as a gift to someone.

@amywilliamsacademy

Made in the USA
Columbia, SC
26 January 2024